Spirit Love

A Memoir of Transformation

Joan Chisholm

Copyright © 2013 by Joan Chisholm

All rights reserved. No part of this book may be reproduced or transmitted in any form or by any means, electronic or mechanical, including photocopying and recording, or by any information storage or retrieval system without written permission from the author, except for brief passages quoted in a review.

The author does not endorse the use of any specific technique in the search for spiritual awareness and intends only to dispense general information. The author and publisher are not responsible for the consequences of any activities you may pursue as a result of reading this book.

Cover painting by John Tate, www.dragonzoo.com

Interior layout by Launchpad Press, www.launchpad-press.com

Published by The Write Milieu
312-550 Queens Quay West
Toronto, Ontario,Canada
m5v 3m8

Library and Archives Canada Cataloguing in Publication Data

Chisholm, Joan, 1946–

Spirit Love: A memoir of transformation / Joan Chisholm
1. Love 2. Spirituality 3. Writing 4. Inspirational
5. Finding and Following Your Dream 6. Motivational

ISBN-13: 978-0-9879884-2-3

Also by Joan Chisholm

Poetry
In *Canadian Voices, Volume 1*
　"Is Love So Fragile?"
　"A Thousand Stars"

In *Canadian Imprints*
　"Elemental"
　"Spirit Love"
　"You and I"

Forthcoming Books, 2014–2015

Love Is the Answer: A Book of Poems about Love, Passion, and Personal Power

Absurd and Ridiculous Books for Children

How I Found Out That the Purpose of My Life Is To Love

Dedication

I dedicate *Spirit Love* to my parents, Thomas and Matilda Martin, who allowed me to fly, and to my siblings. What a journey we are having together.

Thank you all.

Contents

Acknowledgements	ix

Part 1: My Self-Examination   1

Author's Notes	3
Introduction	7
Surrender	15
Three Sessions with My Spiritual Guides	21
Surrender Summary	51
How Unhappy Was I?	53
Emotional Impediments	54
Do What I Say I Want To Do	55
Taking Down the Barricades	56
The Desire to Achieve My Dream Is Always Present	58
How Does Writing Make Me Feel?	60
An Awareness of Self-Love	61
A Momentous Day	62
A State of Readiness	63
Three Dreams	64
Defining Moments	66
An Abundance of Inspiration	72
My Built-in Radar and My Knowing	73
List of Synchronicities	75

Part 2: Your Self-Examination   77

Using Your Talents	79
Who Are You?	81
Avoiding the Void	83
Name Your Dream	85
An Act of Intent	86
Focus Your Desire and Intention	87
Your Body and Emotions in Balance	89
Balance Equals Energy	90
Maintaining the Passion of Your Dream	91
Do It for Yourself	92
Heaven on Earth	94
Love and Happiness	95

Part 3: The End   99

My Exhilaration	101
Souvenirs of Wisdom Received from My Spiritual Guides	104
Creation	114

Acknowledgements

A special thank you to my beautiful sons Graham and Michael, who made me show up for love. To my grandson Maxym, thank you for giving me the clearest view of what it is to be a human. You have given me immeasurable joy!

The most special thanks I give to my husband Peter, who is my personal happiness maker and my greatest supporter.

I also wish to thank my early insightful and sympathetic editor, Makeda Silvera; consultant, Roz Spafford; and coach, Suzanne Cumming. Much appreciation goes to my editor, Caroline Kaiser, for her professional and warm leadership. Her precision with *Spirit Love* was admirable and love itself.

I thank my essential and brave readers: Joan Jones, Dr. John Foulds, Dr. Nicholas Fields, Flavia Cosma, Krista Jensen, Olga Kangun, Andy Turnbull, my sisters Annette Arjoon and Elizabeth Lee, and my brother Michael Max Martin. As well, I thank Marika, Olenka, and Areta Gawrachynsky.

Much gratitude goes to Stefko, who recognized the soul in *Spirit Love*, as well as to Yara Jakymiw for her artistic ideas.

Many thanks to the best cheering squad in the world: my niece and nephew Tilitha and Chaz Arjoon, my sister Sita and her husband Melchior Taylor, my family in love Liz and Brian Dinchong, Denise Fields, Roxanne Fields, Maria Taylor, and Stephen and Bob Jones.

I am indebted to my brother, Dr. Peter (Dino) Martin, and his wife, Mrs. Cheemattee Martin, who sustained me with the reminder of their example that dreams do come true.

And of course, I thank Cathy Primeau, my dearest friend and sister in spirit, for being with me all the way.

My sincerest gratitude goes to all my family and friends who encouraged me with words and to those who were with me in spirit.

Finally, to my angel and my spiritual guides, the energy of my higher spirit or higher self: you are the guiding principles of my life.

I thank you all for your loving support!

> All day I think about it, then at night, I say it. Where did I come from, and, what am I supposed to be doing? I have no idea. My soul is from elsewhere, I am sure of that, and I intend to end up there.
>
> —JALAL AD-DIN RUMI (1207–1273)
> PERSIAN POET AND MYSTIC

PART 1
My Self-Examination

Author's Notes

Answering the Questions

Who am I? What is it that I am supposed to be doing with my life? These are the two seminal questions I have been asking myself since I was eighteen years old.

But a sudden, impending separation from my husband, after twenty-eight years of marriage, forced me to focus my attention on my life and my dreams. My future was at stake, and it was sinking out of sight. My usual optimism had been assaulted. I urgently needed to answer these questions. Thinking of my future, I sought counselling. A question was posed: What am I doing with *my* life? My mind opened itself, allowing me to connect my present unhappiness to the unhappiness I felt in not pursuing my long-held dream of being a writer. Several synchronistic events happened rapidly; one was seeking and finding a different kind of counsellor to help me discover my new life. I wanted to know what kept me from writing when it was all I thought about doing every day of my adult life. This counsellor introduced me to my spiritual guides.

At a young age, I had expressed my individuality by writing poetry and prose sporadically. I was not aware of it at the time, but writing was my natural and earliest attempt to answer my question about the purpose of my life. I began to know myself by reviewing the values and philosophies I have lived by, and the encouragement I gave others to express themselves by using their gifts to live a passionate and fulfilling life. This review helped me to start writing again with greater determination and discipline.

Comforted and encouraged by the detailed help I received from my spiritual guides, I delved further into my writing past. Archeological digs into a box of my early writing gave flesh and bones to my lost dreams. Seeing the evidence of my old passion motivated me to act. I blew on the remaining embers, and the fire of writing was rekindled. I burned away non-writing habits that resisted change. My long-buried dream to become a writer grew in intensity and became real. Memories of my past writing encouraged me to write again and were strengthened by an unseen and powerful organizing mechanism. I sensed that I was being guided.

Spirit Love traces the journey I was compelled to take. It shows the precise steps I took to fulfill and realize my writing dreams. Through daily meditation with my spiritual guides, my focus grew stronger and my desired outcomes became manifest. *Spirit Love* relates how I manifested my passion for living a purposeful and self-fulfilled life.

Below are the questions I asked myself, and the answers gave me the clarity to change from being afraid of being myself to being courageous:

Am I soulfully happy with my life? What would make me soulfully happy?

Do I make choices based only on societal and familial expectations?

Do my choices reflect my true feelings?

Am I living my life based upon who I am?

What are the real and truthful definitions I hold of myself?

Spirit Love is the story of how to access your authentic self. It encourages you to draw a cohesive map of your inner and outer worlds. The map outlines possibilities that were once hidden. *Spirit Love* can show you how to change your existing life for the life you want.

Your dream is your aspiration, your possibility, your hope, and your ideal. It is born from the bountiful and boundless chimera, the wild creativity, of your imagination alone. It's a sure thing!

Our spiritual guides, our angel, and our God or Goddess selves are all waiting to help us. Ask for their help and then follow the intuitive suggestions they offer to you. Take the action necessary to move forward to achieve the life you want. The spiritual help offered comes from a source that replenishes itself eternally.

The greatest discovery I have made is that we are not alone.

Introduction

The Knowing

My earliest, overriding memory was one of "knowing"— knowing that something else existed that I could not see. This aspect of my nature made me into an observer who was always looking for the meaning behind what I heard and saw around me. But it was an unknown "knowing." I sensed that there was something waiting to be known by me.

My Long-Held Dream of Writing

The flickering lights of my dream to be a writer have been blinking on and off in my mind's eye for thirty years. Throughout that time, I have always been conscious of *not* writing. Writing was an elusive dream in my adult life, but I could recall a nascent attempt at writing my first poem about love, an entry for a poetry contest. I was thirteen or fourteen years old, and I won the contest. Much later, when my children were three and one-half and one year old, I began to write again. Joyful stories about our young children's unfolding world and unbridled love poems about my husband emerged. My parents and siblings also sang their songs too in my writing. I studied books on writing, attended readings, journeyed to writing retreats, and registered for courses at the local college. These sporadic activities subdued my bad temper at being unable to say out loud that I secretly and passionately longed to write. Although I was centred and fully happy taking care of my children and husband, managing both the household and helping in the family business, I still felt untethered to my personal reality and adrift from myself during long periods of not writing. This inactivity increased my lack of confidence, and I squandered the available time I had to write. I suffered a loss of self-esteem. *My* innately felt contribution to the world was not being developed. I was unaware that the essential condition for my soulful happiness was to write.

I spent most of my time distracted by my inability to understand why I was not writing. Finally, it occurred to me why I was immobilized with ambivalence. I concluded that *I had no reason to write*—that is, I had no particular writing project to spur me on. I also asked myself, "For whom am I writing?" Writing solely because my mind and body came alive when I expressed ideas and feelings about my life and the world did not occur to me.

Unable to explore ways of moving from the great *desire* I had to write full-time to actually *believing* that writing was a valid activity for me, I waited for someone to encourage me. I placed no expectations of writing on myself. I preferred that someone else believed in my ability to write. I needed permission to write. I also lacked belief in my ability to complete a writing project in which I would have to maintain mental discipline and physical perseverance. Looming larger in my mind was another obstacle: a fear of showing my true feelings to my family and friends about the different ways I thought life could be lived.

Habits: a Shadowing of Family and Society

Growing up, I had absorbed the prevailing tenet in our large family of eleven children that disagreement and acting from self-interest created cracks in the smooth façade of our familial world. No discussion and, therefore, no consensus could be built from the absolute yeas or nays encountered. Scared that the resulting cracks could enlarge into a chasm too wide to cross, I retreated from challenges that might have caused unnecessary disharmony at home. Later, I used this template in my marriage. I became a full-time passive observer of life. By adopting this strategy as an adult, I hampered the creativity that would have connected me with the world outside of myself. Writing would have transformed me into a doer. I was not a doer—I reacted to life.

During the gestation period of my becoming a writer, I used my creativity solely to express love in my homemaker's role. My mother, with wordless eloquence and elegance, had taught me how. In truth, I was comfortable reliving my mother's habit of serenely giving unconditional love to everyone. Her joy in giving was energetic. Two days before Christmas each year, she would spend up to six hours a day sewing new curtains for every window in the house and then fall ill from exhaustion between Christmas and New Year's Eve. Her love was transcendent as she calmly offered it to her husband and eleven children. I absorbed it all. Over time I unwittingly slipped into sacrifice and martyrdom. No one had demanded it of me. Long after it was unnecessary to tend the hearth unceasingly, I continued to do so, as I could not bear to think why I was not writing.

Creating happiness for other people was always my first consideration. Creating happiness for *me* was my last concern. I imagined accruing brownie points because of my desire to please others, and that I'd ensured protection from the big bad world for myself. When I was growing up in the sixties, power and authority at home and in the business world were overwhelmingly allowed only to men, and I, as a female, perceived the world as unbalanced. Although I was fairly sure of myself, I still saw no clear ways of building experiences to bolster my confidence in those areas.

Rethinking the Landscape and Making the Transition

During my long period of motherhood, I would ask myself, "Am I ready to do the only thing that not doing undermines my happiness each day?" I would answer, "Yes, yes, a thousand times yes!" Then I would slog through the mud fields of my mind, thinking ambiguous but passionate thoughts about writing. To overcome the futility of trying to walk through that difficult terrain, I praised myself: at least I was staying in the right arena by taking courses and completing writing assignments. Additionally, I was mired in my own questions about whether I was a homemaker or a writer. I believed I had to make a choice to be one or the other; I saw the choices as mutually exclusive.

As time passed, I became less centred on propelling my dreams into reality, although the heady swirl I felt whenever a creative urge forced me to write never left me. My self-esteem suffered, and I was brought to my knees by the added stress of a menopause that heightened my emotional responses. I was overcome by indecisiveness and near tears whenever I felt provoked by my loved ones. More self-confidence drifted away from me. The routines of the day seemed boring, and each morning loomed as a challenge to my happiness. Instead of writing each day, I placed all of my creative energy into the job of being a wife and mother. I gardened ferociously and imagined a better relationship with my husband—all the while riding the constant waves of my children's teenage angst. Life with two teenagers did not help me find the clarity I needed. I was fearful of the future and emotionally tired from being unable to move toward the wholeness I was seeking. I was only living half of my life.

Underlying all of these thoughts was the knowledge that I wanted to write—that I could write. I wore a mask of sadness, and it was unbearable to look in the mirror. I did not have the determination to do the one thing I wanted to accomplish in my life. Dusty boxes of embryonic writing lay silently, waiting to be born. Inertia to feed the hunger in my heart sidelined any motivation I had left for more studies at the local college.

When the spectre of a separation appeared after twenty-eight years of marriage, I looked at writing as a serious occupation for the first time.

Seeking a Different Kind of Counsellor

Although I was deeply conscious of pursuing my dream, I was simultaneously afraid of tackling it. I approached my desk many times and turned away without attempting to sit down and write. I became aware that I needed to talk to a counsellor—a different kind of counsellor—who would help me integrate my internal world—what my spirit wanted—with my external world.

The New Me

I finally met that spiritual counsellor. A friend introduced me to someone who had the gift to connect me to my spiritual guides. The purpose of this connection was to allow me to receive the spiritual help that I requested. I wanted answers as to why I did not write.

I received three counselling sessions with my spiritual guides. The effect on me was profound; I was catapulted into the unknown and mysterious world I always thought existed. The counselling I received validated my desire to live the true purpose of my life. I also received countless suggestions generously given about my health and happiness.

I immediately became acutely aware of my surroundings and noticed the sun shining on the water in the fountain at the back of the garden and the fragrance dispersing from the lavender when it shook in the breeze. Birdsong thrilled my heart, and I savoured only delicious foods that were healthy for my body. My mind began to release negative thoughts. I lived in the moment and made decisions that created a different harmony in our family during a tumultuous time. I felt compassion for everyone in our new family situation and found solace in the beauty around me. I felt gratitude for just being alive. I became a full participant in my life. I was no longer a passive observer. A commitment to make my dreams come true became a natural extension of my new state of being. I instinctively and powerfully wanted to move ahead to share my writing with the world.

SPIRIT LOVE—A SPECIFIC WRITING PROJECT

Spirit Love was born. I focused all my attention on the work of writing and completed the first draft in four months. In my mind's eye, the act of writing reminded me of a photograph of my younger son, bare chested and in a diaper, clenching his toes on a sandy beach on the Toronto Islands. He had decided, at that moment, to take a step—he was venturing into the unknown. His toes curled under to hold the sand still—he was making a stable foundation. His tiny shoulders and body twisted slightly to steady his balance—he was preparing for unpredictable events. His fists clenched—he was adding concrete to his efforts. Finally, he dragged one foot from behind him and placed it slightly ahead of his body—he was developing momentum. As he inched forward to his goal of walking, portraits of his earlier efforts were embedded in the sand behind him in an uneven trail. He landed on his bottom several times, and when he retrieved the memory of his earlier successes, he rose from his seated position to try again. Once more, he stick-handled his way to move further along on the beach and, inevitably, he walked.

MY DREAM CAME TRUE

During my writing journey, my focus was sometimes derailed by personal crises that delayed the progress of *Spirit Love*. Nevertheless, when I had to make decisions, I always asked myself, "What would love do?" The right answers would come to me, unerringly, as I looked through the prism of love at others and myself. The consequences of my actions later showed me that I had made the best decisions.

When I conceived my dream, I was saying, "I believe in me!" I was born from a magically mixed bag of DNA that created a unique me. My genome contained all the ingredients of the essence of my creative force. When I sought to uncover my special talent and divined the words that I hoped would benefit others, the ecstasy I felt in doing what I love infused my entire life. Writing, as with any creative outpouring, is my fervent desire to manifest something of meaning from nothing that existed before.

SURRENDER

ACKNOWLEDGING MY SPIRITUAL SIDE

Feeling alone and afraid in a desert and thirsty to pursue my dream, I was propelled to ask more questions. I suddenly remembered the biblical exhortations, "Seek and you shall find," and "Knock and the door shall be opened." If I did not knock on the door, it wouldn't be opened and I wouldn't be able to access the answers I sought from within. In the context of my internal life, I was an explorer seeking new realms. When I finally knocked, I surrendered to the unknown.

I felt completely alone as I fought to find the true meaning of my existence and how it related to my dream. I wished to stop living outside of myself and to live as a human who was *being*—and not only living from the outer layer, the visible parts, alone. I wanted to enrich my life and live also from the layers below that contained the elemental and organic grains that were nourishing and delicious. I believed that living with the knowledge of my inner and outer worlds was the bedrock of a soulful life. I knew that paying attention to the details of this potpourri would invoke my soul.

Almost immediately, practical and spiritual help appeared.

Spiritual and Practical Acts of Surrender

A Spiritual Act—Hearing from My Angel

One night, drained by the anguish of being unable to see the larger view of my future, I directly implored no one in particular: "I need help; please help me."

I heard a voiceless response quietly but clearly in my conscious mind: "I am your angel, and I'm with you."

The reply stunned me with its simplicity and clarity. I could not identify the speaker as male or female. I heard only a voice. Relief descended on me: I would not have to go through life unable to call on someone to help me answer the deeper questions I had been asking. I felt comforted knowing that I was not alone.

This experience compelled me to ask for more answers from the unseen world.

I slept well that night and, within my soul-self, my happiness remained constant from that day on.

*A Practical Act—
Writing a Letter to My Angel*

Soon after hearing from my angel, while sitting at my desk one silent, solitary morning, I wrote this letter of despair about my inability to commit to writing. This was my Garden of Gethsemane, my moment of anguished contemplation:

Dear Angel,

I am speaking to you, my own angel. I want to ask you a direct question. You know that I am hurting inside. The hurt lingers just below the surface of my life. All discussions about why I am not writing I take personally. I try to overcome this reaction by studying and practising self-esteem. But mental ropes hold me back. I approach my writing desk and turn away before I can sit and write.

I have more questions for you, dear angel, my constant companion. What is it that keeps throwing me off, so easily, from writing? My family registers their disappointment at my failed attempts to write each day. They are impatient with comments about uncompleted projects and watch silently as I fumble and struggle each day that I do not write. One of my sons confessed that he does not know what to tell his friend's mother when she asks, "What is your mother doing?" I cried, as I realized I still had not let my dream out into the world, even though my passion for writing was strong within me.

I feel anguish at my failures. What I hate more than failing, dear angel, is being criticized. I rationalize my anger, disappointment, and tears by believing my family wants me to be perfect. But is it that I want me to be perfect? Am I the one who criticizes me? Am I disappointed at not expressing my ideas and beliefs clearly?

My jumbled, mumbled half-thoughts are marred by fear of being judged. Dear angel, these challenging aspects of my writing life made me cry all morning. The editors in my head are slowly killing my creativity. I do not want it to die. I am alive with life. Life is now magical, dear angel, with you in it!

A Practical Act—Attending a Seminar

A week later, my intuition drew me to a seminar about organizing a writing project, so I attended the one-day event. I learned how to structure a writing idea by first giving names to each chapter. I could produce an organized overview of everything I needed to develop the idea. Maintaining a simple and direct format, I then named the relevant topics that I could cluster within each chapter. To expand these topics further, I answered the questions: who, what, where, why, and when? Following this process eliminated writer's block. I could parachute my ideas into the corresponding topic in any chapter, and with the necessary research, still maintain order in the manuscript.

The question was what I would write about. The meaningful answer was to write about the experience of following my dream. I would write about the philosophies I held about truth and self-love, including the spiritual help I received, and show how these philosophies led me to take hold of following my dream and passion.

This structured approach to writing allowed me to complete the first draft of *Spirit Love* in four months of writing five to six hours per day.

Spiritual Help—An Introduction to My Spiritual Guides and My Three Sessions with Them

During a yearly hiking weekend with a group of female friends, I mentioned to one of them that I believed I needed to find a different kind of counsellor for questions I had about my life. I said to her that perhaps I needed to talk to a spiritual counsellor. Remarkably, she knew of one.

The information I received over fifteen months from the three sessions with my spiritual guides allowed me to know and accept myself completely through the perspective of love. The sessions brought gentle and loving reminders of my tendencies and acknowledgments of my desires to the forefront where I could accept them. They also contained detailed ideas for advancing my dream of being a writer. They advised me to sit at the computer and begin writing, and that a project would present itself to me. And so it did. But there was an inherent paradox to my "writing project" since I started to write it without knowing precisely what the topic would be.

What follows are the three sessions I had with my spiritual guides through my spiritual counsellor.

Three Sessions with My Spiritual Guides

Session 1

Note: What follows has been adapted from the original transcripts. The spiritual guides are speaking through the counsellor, who writes down what they have to communicate.

> Counsellor. I ask to be protected in this medium of communication as I seek guidance for Joan. I ask for God, Goddess, Higher Spirit, or Great Spirit to come to me and protect us in a circle of light.

> Guides. And so it is. Do not be concerned—the left-leaning feeling means you are working to be in harmony with a higher energy. Your body feels as if it is twisted, but it is not; the two energies are still working to be in harmony. Counsellor, we can use your fingers for this communication.

And we say to you, Joan, all that you already know, all that you already feel, and all that you feel lurking, just under the surface. And so it is not odd that this was your feeling before beginning. Not everyone hears, sees, dreams, and knows. Well, everyone is capable of these things, but not everyone makes use of the capacity. For some people, it is a little scary to use it; for others, it is just too far outside their material-based understanding of life. If things are not tangible, they do not believe in them. This is commonplace, but you, Joan, are someone who hears, believes, sees, and is able; you have developed the skills quite consciously and purposefully. You have not accomplished this through reading, but through *feeling* in a way that is not material-based.

Today, Joan, you feel tired of just feeling, of just knowing, and you want to do something with it, so it is time to take action. So what is the problem, Joan? What hinders that step out onto the page? Why this fear? Is it fear of being right, fear of not being right, fear of not being noticed, fear of not being published, fear of not being read—shall we go on? The fears are tremendous and they are unwarranted, but that does not prevent them from recurring again and again. Always, as you know, the fear raises its head and you falter.

Seeking this message, this guidance, is another fear-based action; you fear that what you know is not acceptable. We are not criticizing you for seeking affirmation or confirmation. Rather, we want you to become more confident that what you know, see, hear, and are ready to write onto the page is valid and acceptable. Your words need only be sanctioned by you. They do not need the verification of others. And so, Joan, it is time to take action and write about all the things that you hold in your heart.

You will find that when you review those pieces that you refer to as "stop and start" that among them is the basis of a body of work, so set about rereading them, editing them, and going forward with what feels right. No one writes everything all at the same time, no one—not even those who say that they do and pretend that they have. Therefore, whatever you have written is worthy of resuscitation. Resuscitate all of these stop-and-start pieces and examine them for their intrinsic value. All that you write is valuable and worthy, even if you edit it into another creation. It served as the catalyst for your final product, of which there are none. You will edit the same work over and over until the book itself is produced, and then you will edit it even while it is on the shelves of bookstores.

Release your ego, Joan; ego concerns keep you in a place of stagnation. Ego makes things not feel very sweet. Maybe somewhere there is greener grass, a better atmosphere for writing, and more peace and quiet. You feel that if only there were not these issues to deal with, then your mind would be clear and you would be able to write; you find reasons not to. There are many more reasons to write than you could concoct not to write, or to explain why you do not write.

Your family will move into support mode as soon as you take yourself seriously. They too are waiting to support you. They do not criticize. They may feel that they are being supportive by questioning. Your insecurity makes you receive this with rancour. You ask, "Why are you criticizing me?" One day, Joan, you will not care that much about what every single person says or thinks about you. You will then be happier, for you will care only what spirit says to you and how you think about yourself.

Your first big job is to learn to love yourself much better. Value yourself and take pride in yourself—even just for breathing. It is the start. Then move to the next baby step in appreciating yourself—appreciate where you *are* from where you *were*. Give yourself accolades for every single little thing that you do, but see that you do not bore others with accolade-giving because then it will be an exercise in ego. As soon as you begin to demand that others engage in this assuaging of spirit, you are being insecure. Love yourself; do it well, and be quiet about it.

By suggesting you love yourself, we are not suggesting that you engage in excessive pampering. Rather, we are speaking of internal messages of love: "Joan, you are wonderful," "I love and approve of you, Joan," "I am here for you, in all ways," and "I may not have been there for you before this, but I am here for you now, and I will always be here for you, Joan." Repeat these messages every single day upon waking and see if you do not feel the results. This is simplicity and effectiveness to the highest degree.

Loving the self also includes considering how you nurture your gifts, and how you keep your promises to yourself. Maintain integrity with yourself, and you will feel a great sense of accomplishment. Set yourself small goals so that you do not end up with none or only a few of your objectives met or you will feel disappointed in yourself, as if what you have done is an exercise in futility. A small goal may be to get a pen and pad, or a computer disk, and be ready to write daily. Your first goal is to get prepared with the tools, nothing more.

You do not need weeks and weeks of quiet, and you do not need to announce to the whole world, including family members, that you are getting ready to write. Make it personal, between you and your God-self. When you are ready, write. Write whatever comes to your mind first and foremost.

And stay with it, writing your way into the centre. Sometimes, you are not quite connected to your inner core, so you must write your way to it. Writing will enable you to make this journey. See writing as a way to move yourself into your centre, and then write from that place.

There is much support available to you from your family. They may be disappointed at the moment, but all will get over it. You too are feeling disappointed in yourself—it's neither necessary nor justified. The disappointment in both you and others is ego based—all are concerned that you have not accomplished your heart's desire. But all of you will get over it.

Most importantly, you need to release these feelings of low self-worth linked to not having done what you thought you would do. Life marches on. Release all of that and begin again, as if you were fresh from a harvest of deep introspection and have now come to the edge of the top of the hill, having climbed from the bottom. There, you can see the sun rise and set. You can see vast expanses of land, and you can dream.

At the top of the hill, you can finally feel your feet firmly on the ground. You can feel the heights to which you've always wanted your spirit to take you. And they're good heights, far from the earthbound considerations that pull you down to the bottom. Now there is no scrambling up the hill, for your soul winged its way there, carrying you along with it. There is space to move your arms about, feel the air, and let the sun kiss your face. And now you can write.

Many more things are connected to the body and the heart, but you tire.

[*My guides pause for a moment to allow my counsellor to rest. My counsellor repeats the initial invocation, asking for God, Goddess, Higher Spirit, or Great Spirit to provide protection for us both in a circle of light as she seeks guidance for me.*]

GUIDES. And so it is. Always, it is good to ask for protection, blessing, and guidance; it eases the communication and keeps all things in this way of light, reason, and understanding. The harmony between the two energy systems is now better, and you felt this, hence your desire, counsellor, to continue to allow the writing to take place.

Joan, you are quite a spiritually elevated person, on a higher plane than you acknowledge. You are able to read people quite well. This is a boon for a writer, Joan, so go to it with gusto. This is how you would spur on others, so it is appropriate that we speak to you thus. You are quite good at motivating others, as you will admit to yourself, but you ask yourself, "Why can I encourage others and not myself?" Encouraging others is easier to do, Joan, just as it is perhaps easier for you to give than to receive.

Give yourself high marks for having come thus far and for still having a memory of what you wanted to do; that in itself is an accomplishment in listening and paying attention. Joan, you do listen to what you want deep inside, but you do not always manage to sort it out. The reason? It's time to organize the whole process, Joan; regularize and ritualize all things, and all things will then be possible. "Only believe" is a saying that has become trite, but it is decidedly true. All things are possible if you only believe. You can accomplish your heart's desire by putting it at the centre of your energy system and praying for help to enable it to come into being. It's simple, and it is a play in five parts.

Make the first part your acceptance that indeed you can write, and that what you have to say is valuable and worth committing to paper. Forget about whether or not others will find it worthy. Eventually, they will. Although we do not engage in fortune-telling, it is necessary to tell you, Joan, that what you have to say on paper is needed, useful, and desirable to others.

And now we return to the ritualized methods that will

enable what you desire to come into being. Write every day, Joan—every single day. Write with your whole heart, not thinking of what others will think of what you have written. Write even if you think what you have to say is not something that sounds profound and earth-shattering. Just write it down anyway.

Some days, all you will write is the one sentence. So be it. Other days, all you will write is an additional word in that sentence; you may simply edit the sentence. Nonetheless, you will be keeping in touch with your writing, and the spirit of the work will come to you and bless you daily, enabling you to write more and more.

Sometimes, a work won't feel like what you wish to work on at a given moment. This does not mean that you should abandon it. Sometimes the spirit of the work is in recess. We do not mean to pun, but we say this for emphasis. You too will be suddenly in recess, so do what you do in a recess? You play. You work on other writing that eases your spirit. And the next day you'll return to the initial work, and sometimes to the second work. But never do you not write.

And you always pray. Every single morning before you speak with others, you pray. You ask your spirit to come to you, bless you, guide you, and help you, every single morning. And in the evening, you say thank you for all that has manifested in your writing, and in your life, for that matter. And you keep on keeping on with the works that make sense to you, every single day.

You write for you and for your spirit only, and you do not engage in what delays or annihilates your writing. Do not give your writing to a critical reader; find a supportive, biased reader, and let that person read what they are prepared to and give you the desired positive feedback. Eventually, you will find editors who will be clinical and skillful, and from them you will receive the hard knocks. But for now, you seek only a supportive reader; that may be you.

It is important to clear the space in which you write, but you needn't be dramatic about it—there's no need to change it entirely. But you do need to make colours easy on the heart and on the eye. While we are not suggesting any major overhauls, we are suggesting that you let more light in however you can—nothing dramatic. Perhaps the curtains are heavy and dark, and there are wooden walls, in which case you could hang something gold. You need gold around you, deep corn or yellow-gold, in flowers, a wall hanging, or a bed sheet on which you sleep for a week or two. Yellow-gold should be a permanent colour in your writing space so that it feels like the sun every time you walk in. You are not necessarily comfortable wearing this colour, but it is a splendid colour on which to feast your eyes, and you will enjoy having its vibration in your space. You need its creative, intellectual energy constantly, but especially when you are trying to connect with the spirit within that helps you to write. Bring yellow flowers, daisies, or daffodils, into the space when possible. Although you might have it in something permanent, like a cushion or a wall hanging, you could have it in flowers as well.

Eating some yellow foods is also good—an orange each day, yellow plums, and yellow corn maybe a few times each week. You don't need to be fanatical and have all yellow foods on your plate. You do go overboard with things. You have too much stress and dissipate too much energy on being perfect in all things, but no one is perfect.

You have an allergy to dust. Wipe all dust with a slightly damp cloth so that it does not fly up and tickle your nose. Dust is very bad for you. You are also allergic to mouldy things, and there are some present in your environment. It's easy to identify and easy to dispense with it. Your plants are not really thriving in the dampness, but are merely keeping mould present. Identify where there is mould. Clearing it away will increase the depth and quality of your sleep quite considerably. Eating and drinking things that make mould is also an issue. Wine, bread, cake, muffins, biscuits, nuts, mushrooms, and red meat are all problems for you.

These few things mentioned will enable you to make some great changes, if you are able to attend to them over a period of time. There's no need to do all things at the same time. It is necessary, though, for you to begin to write today, Joan. And get up tomorrow and write again—not a journal, but a real project. Just sit and begin and the project will make itself known to you. Have no expectations; just be happy to release these words onto the page daily. After some time, look at what you have written and you will recognize where you are headed. You will see it as if you are looking at a panorama. Thank you.

Session 2

Guides: And so be it, and so it is, always and forevermore. Always, Joan, we are here to protect, guide you, and nurture you. We are not *we* in the Earth-school sense of the term. We are of you, Joan, in that we are of the higher energy of your being—your higher spirit and your higher self. We harmonize with the counsellor's energy and with her use of her fingers. We use her fingers to speak to you of those things that we do normally in both the dream state and in the waking state of your daily life. We are not entities in the usual sense, nor are we earthly guides of the Earth's beings; we are not people, with heads, mouths, and limbs. We are, however, *of* the entities of the Earth, for all earthly entities have energy parts of their being that harmonize with other like energies, and thus it is that we can speak here using the fingers of the writer to communicate what we would have been saying to you in other mediums—through dreams, or in a certain sense of knowing or in a way of seeing, being able to discern the real in the illusions that abound.

Joan, first and foremost, you are not alone. Sometimes you think you are, even in a crowd of people. You are alone in one sense, yes, that is, as a total being, but not on the material plane. The spirit part of the being is always with you; your soul is always with you, and spirit is the energy that enables the soul to fulfill its mission on the earthly plane, enabling the body to fulfill its mission. Joan, what is your mission? You wonder this. Are you not fulfilling your mission, Joan? We would say that you have been, and you are performing it well.

And you are aware of the nature of that mission. To see what it is, you must look around you at what you have accomplished and are continuing to accomplish. Remember that you are not a one-dimensional being; you are multifaceted, and as such, you are doing well. You sometimes want to put your head into a one-dimensional place, but you will soon be unhappy there. We feel sure that you will know what we mean when we say that to be one thing does not mean you must forsake the other things. You are many things, and many parts of many things.

And we must hasten to add, however, that we do not recommend martyrdom, since that is not what we are addressing. We are, however, acknowledging an unasked question about how you are to conduct your life now, in terms of both time and substance. You are wavering in between the two, as if there is a battle between them, but there is none.

Joan, it is a good idea to see all things as being substance, and nothing is unworthy of attention. However, this does not mean that you should deny yourself the freedom to be who you are in this configuration of all things. All things includes you, Joan, your soul, your heart, your desires—all of who you are. There is no way to live without acknowledging you as the centre, you as the nexus of just who Joan is. We would hope this is clear.

We would also like to mention, Joan, that it is time for you to move the things that cause you to feel pressure to a place where they won't. The things that arrive in your life as pressure should not be allowed to arrive any more. We cannot be more specific, but we will respond to the counsellor's query as to what these things are. Joan, suddenly, just as you are sailing smoothly along, issues arrive which do not concern you in a big way, and you find yourself stopping to deal with them even though they are not even interesting. Well, Joan, your challenge is how to not allow these things to completely disturb your equilibrium, as indeed they do.

Now, Joan, you will find new and innovative ways of renegotiating relationships, movements, and change in your life. You will need to do this in order not to be so apprehensive of these changes.

Arrival and departure is a great concern to you—arrival and departure of things and people that are not willed by you. Well, Joan, you will find balance, and finding it makes it possible to harmonize with others. Find balance, and there is no need to go to extremes of determining a new way of being. Sometimes, the new way of being is the way to go, but always seek balance. When your heart says, "No more," you will know that you have given all you can. This is not yet a way of being for you, and it is not the way you would have things go. But, Joan, your heart will tell you, and when it does, you will not need to feel anything but the greatest blessing for a life well worth saving—your own. Saving yourself will always be available to you, in or out of any relationship. Nothing is worth giving all that is within you to try to save things that can't be saved. They can, however, always be healed.

We are saying, attend to a healing—your own—and then all things will be clear. We are aware that we have spoken somewhat cryptically, but it is the way we could be as clear as possible without being fortune-tellers, since this is not our way. We wish to be as helpful as possible. Joan, you strive very hard and you know that there is always a way to be happy. Your strong point is being able to reach for happiness at all times. Others are not always blessed with so positive an outlook.

Joan, is there a compromise you can achieve within which you can function? If so, then how can you achieve it? And if the answer to those questions makes you feel that you are not interested in finding such a resolution, then you will have answered a big question of your own and done so on your own.

We are always seeking to present choices and not fortune-telling. In this situation, we would suggest that you fill your life with what makes you happy and to do it from a place of good relationships. You can also make a decision not to compromise, and then, Joan, you would be living a very different life. You would need to embrace this decision fully, being cognizant of all of the parameters. The way is never that clear-cut, but nor is it strewn with thorns. It is, however, full of learning and realization. From your experience will come the wisdom to know the right way.

To arrive at a place of centredness where such knowing is available, we would suggest that you consciously seek to be even more centred than you are now. You have gained much confidence; continue to walk on this uphill road with power and with love. As you already do, always keep love in the equation and act from a place of love, Joan. Be more centred, more in tune with all of who you are. Being more balanced comes from being more centred, and being more centred means that you make all decisions from the core of your being.

Centring yourself more, Joan, will allow you to hear more fully what is overtaking you and making you feel stifled. It will allow you to step outside of this and feel the passion within you that still needs to be released. The writing will always flow, Joan—of this you can be sure. Indeed, from a place of disgruntlement, writing will flow even more easily, for it is at the writing table that you can sort, analyze, and put things right. You can put anything right in writing—no pun intended.

We now feel a lot of confusion and confused images, which show you sitting at your desk, and other energies hovering over and around you, as if the area around you needs to be grounded—not just you. Yes, the area needs to be cleared and cleansed, for within it are raised voices. The messages, intent, and feelings remain; they hover as energy that you are reading. You can see to this by clearing the space every day with cleansing things for the air. Joan, light a white candle and say some prayers in your writing space. Counsellor, as you believe, all writing ought to begin with prayer. Indeed, it will help you immensely, Joan, to say a prayer to dispel the negative energy in the writing space. Also, Joan, the air itself could stand purification. See to it—you know what to do. White flowers in the writing space are a good idea as well, and you will love that. Put cut flowers there when you are able, Joan, or a white flowering plant.

The space does indeed need neutralizing, but this is peripheral to your broader needs, which we will deal with in a moment. For neutralizing the writing space, we would suggest you bring in a fountain, one that is either quiet or noisy, according to what you can stand, Joan. Your images in the fountain ought to be of the sacred and images that appeal to you. We would suggest that cleaning the fountain, changing the water for the flowers, trimming the candle, and lighting it when all is ready become a ritual for you. You will have a great sense of peace, Joan, and you will treasure these moments. See that you attend to this ritual before you talk to others as the day begins.

White is a good colour for you to use to neutralize, heal, and shift energy. We don't mean healing of the body, but healing of the feelings. White sheets would help, Joan, but they are not a necessity, merely a suggestion. You could use green sheets as well, for peace and calm. We would also suggest that you drink water sufficiently, sipping it rather than drinking it in a continuous motion.

The prayers you say each day, Joan, will include all that is in your heart about life, relationships, writing, the soul, the spirit, joy, appreciation, and happiness. Recognize that these prayers will be your own, created to suit your particular state of being. Your prayers will correspond to experience, and no standard one will always do the trick, for you may have a yearning in your heart on a given day and the usual prayer will not apply.

Your yearning can be brought into prayer daily, making it more heartfelt than hitherto experienced. You will feel as if you are praying for the first time, and indeed, it will be a first time in terms of depth. Each time, Joan, the depth you reach will be that much greater depending on your place in your spirit-walk. Now, you need to go deeper, to feel deeper, and to reach deeper. The spirit of the work is already there waiting, Joan; it will move to greet you, and the work itself will flow more smoothly than it already has.

Lack of water is a concern. You know this, Joan, but you forget sometimes, and then it becomes serious. It is not so much a lack of water as it is a need to dilute your palate, and water will help to do that. Joan, you will understand, even if you don't, counsellor.

Joan, contemplate flowers as they grow and in vases. Strange, you think, counsellor, but it is very relevant to what you, Joan, are working on now. It will enable you to understand a particular bump in the work. The image you hold of gazing at flowers for a long time is precisely correct. Sometimes, Joan, you should write at different locations; it makes for a change in environment and more of a feeling of peacefulness. Go to a place where you can gaze at flowers—take your notebook and write while gazing at them. A painting of a flower will help, but it is not the same thing, as it is not real.

Light is what I see now—white walls and white lace curtains blowing in the breeze, and white cotton covering things. What you are seeing, counsellor, is Joan's space and the white fabric she will spread on a table. White is a good neutralizing agent as the colour is flat, and this is useful to you, Joan. However, it is not your predominant colour, and you know which colours are right for you on a given day. Go with that knowledge, Joan.

Your health issues are not profoundly disturbed by the lack of water, but they soon could be. Sleep is also disturbed by your need for water. The headaches are caused too by a need for daily movement outside where you live, so that there is less pressure on the head. You need less time in the one environment.

Joy is needed, Joan. Make joy. It's a simple statement, but it will have great meaning. When you make joy for you, then you will make joy for everyone. You are much in need of it, and it will make you feel that you are thriving, and so you will be. "I am joyful" should be said daily, Joan. When you say it, so it is.

You have a feeling of emptiness, Joan, so fill up the space. Make or paint art. Fill up the emptiness with flowers, colour, artistic things, music, and laughter. Do not let these grey colours spread like a blanket over the colours of your life.

These few things will help you, we hope, at this time. Thank you.

Session 3

GUIDES: And so be it, and so it is, always and forevermore. As always, Joan, we are here to protect, nurture, and guide you. We are here as your wellspring of nurturing. That is not an understatement. Joan, you need a wellspring of nurturing that will not leave you needing succor, kindness, gentleness, and loving words, given freely; there should be no sparing use of these things.

It is important, Joan, for you to avidly seek this kind of nurturing. Seek it where the wellspring is always available, where there is no dearth of nurturing. Joan, you need to be touched, loved, held, and allowed to release much of the sadness you are harbouring in your heart and body, in all of who you are. You are enveloped in this sadness, and it can be quite devastating if you are not fed with the milk of human kindness. Yes, counsellor, we hear your surprise, and we are trying to be light. We want you, Joan, to smile when you read this. At the same time, we mean to be serious, for it is very important.

Joan, you need to be touched with the loving arms of a mother or someone who will fill that role. That is the kind of loving that comes from a wellspring, for a mother's love never dries up. So, Joan, seek this in another human being immediately and without shame, and say, "I am here to receive loving kindness, for I am no longer able to be without it." Then, Joan, you will receive it, and you will see that you needed to have it; we cannot stress this enough.

This is the main point that we wish to make concerning you, Joan. We are well aware that several sources of this kind of deep, continuous loving is available to you, and you need only ask for it to receive it. You tend not to ask for this kind of loving from mother figures. Joan, now is the time to do so. Let go of all fear of rejection and ask the mother figures in your life for this kind of nurturing.

Ideally, Joan, you would be happy being allowed to cry, for the tears are repressed, and that does not help. Seek and find a place to cry in an organized way. We do not jest. Find a place where you will release all the repressed tears, transforming them into joyful energy again. It is possible. Joan, this is the way to transcend this period. There is no anger, hate, or acrimony. There is, however, deep resentment, and you are too good to allow that resentment to surface. But it remains and now is the time to find a place where you can express it and let it go. Let it go you must, for these nuggets cause the sadness to stay with you and become a chronic thing. Joan, let the sadness go as soon as you are able. Do not stifle it; rather, bring it onto the table and examine it. Write it away from you and out of you.

Also find a person who will listen to it and enable its release. This person will simply give you love, feed you, kiss your cheek, and call you "child" and "dear." This person possesses the wellspring of nurturing. The person who will enable the release of the sadness is a different resource altogether.

We are being very directive, for we sense an urgency in your journey; there is the need for speed.

With this release, you will be a different person, one who others will gladly employ. This is a time for gay colours surrounding you and also a time for much peace. It is sad to shift life, but this shift is toward peace, and that is worthy of celebration.

As you seek a place where you will rest your head and that of your child, look at the environment, keeping in mind the peace you wish to be part of. That is, Joan, seek a place where peace is a standard part of the environment. Everything else will fall into place nicely. Your new home will be nothing short of miraculous. Everything surrounding it will reverberate in the realm of the miraculous. As you order, design, and build in your heart and in your spirit, you will see it manifest in the material, outer realm.

And so, Joan, build inside immediately—visualize your home, visualize your life, and watch it come into being. This is the way with all things: we merely remind you how to create what you desire.

Let the universe be your canvas, and manifest onto it all that your heart desires. Your job, home, life, and peace—all of these things are yours by right. You must accept that in your heart and move to make it happen.

We speak not lightly; we speak with assurance, Joan. Let that sense of assurance be yours in an almost taken-for-granted way. We do not mean that you will become arrogant about what you are able to manifest. On the contrary, you are a humble soul. Rather, we are saying that it is possible to manifest things easily, and that you will merely say to yourself, "I am now ready to accept X in my life," and you will watch it be so.

Joan, this is not a thing to be taken lightly; rather, be proud of this strong faith, for that is what it is.

If fear dares to knock on your door, say, "I am a woman of faith. I release all fear." And then, Joan, redouble your faith-based thinking and see it manifest. All that your heart desires will manifest, for that is what you came here to do. Sometimes, these things sound as if they are in the realm of fantasy; however, we do not do make-believe. Joan, you have the capacity to make manifest your home, work, and life companion situations. For you, these things are simple, requiring no great work. This is but a bump in the road, a most creative bump from which will come all that you could possibly desire. Joan, when things occur, regard them as bumps in the road and ask to be blessed with their transformation into situations that continue to secure your good.

It is time for you to have it all, Joan—peace, happiness, joy, and great love. This is the way to the heart opening up, and it should not be denied to you or anyone else in the Earth school. You are a spirit who loves easily, and now you will love yourself in a much closer, more fulfilling way than you have before. It is not a simplistic thing that we speak of—nor is it complex. You can accomplish much, which you do not recognize, Joan. Now, with the shift in your life, you will accomplish much in another arena. You have already accomplished much with your family. Take a bow, Joan. You have done well.

And now, on to the next task in your life—doing well with Joan. Take a bow for that as well, for you will see that you can develop yourself in ways that will astound you. Indeed, you have already begun, and perhaps you have felt pleased. Now, on to the next leg.

We see that you are in a state of sunny expectation at times. Mornings bring this feeling; allow it.

Think of the sun, Joan, and bring it into your life through yellow when you are not able to turn your face up to the sun. Yellow will bring that feeling to you. It is a bright yellow, bright as the sun. Keep it close to you so that your eyes can feast on it. The yellow of the sun has always been a good thing for you. You don't need to wear it on your body, though you can; it is a colour that your eyes need.

You also need to enhance this colour's energy in your system. Visualize it and bring it into your body. As it courses through, your body will feel wonderful, Joan. You can do it for five minutes or a half-hour. We seek to augment yellow in the colour wheel for you. Gazing at the yellow flame of candles will clear the emotional body and the energy body; both are filled with sadness.

Seek other natural ways to cleanse sadness, Joan, so that your body does not internalize it; this is a big issue for you. The release of sadness and emergence of resentment are closely linked. There is sadness in your son too; he hides it well.

Joan, you are more able now to discern all that is taking place in your life. This is a growth step, coming from the change you have made in your inner vision. It is enhanced, and we welcome that. Our communication with you, of course, is clearer. We are aware that you know this, Joan: we merely state it here to say, "Good girl!"

You are more connected to the source of your power than ever before, and it comes from your diligent reaching to change. You are open to change, which is positive and something you need to be aware of. It is a strength and one of the things that will endear you to an employer.

Now, Joan, it is good to see that you are raising the vibration in your life, space, and environment. Good girl—continue to do so, child, as this is very useful. In addition, continue to see the space as a blessed place, for in it, you grew, created, loved, and journeyed. These are all good movements and experiences.

There are no regrets, so let go as easily as possible, without rancour. You will not be sorry that you are so amenable to releasing, letting go, and not clinging. More importantly, not exercising anger will be a good thing to celebrate later—it is a triumph of transcendence.

You need to release some things you ingest, to relinquish a few things that are causing minor toxicity. Joan, look at your diet carefully and see what you have added that can be released. The problem is a new addition, not an old habit. Water also clears the physical body, and we recommend it as well. Drinking it will make you feel much better and more energized. Moreover, it will raise the vibration of the sacred in your body; at the same time, you will raise this vibration in your living environment, which is needed now more than ever, Joan.

Raising the vibration will ensure that the space remains peaceful for the duration of your time there. Take nothing for granted—your situation is one of great tension. The tension is not because of conflict, but because of the ending of something, or the shifting and changing of it. That this causes tension is understandable, and all parties have tension.

We suggest that you bring some flowers into the space sometimes, and that you do some conscious work to maintaining the sacred vibration there. The flowers ought to be white, Joan. They will make you smile and breathe a sigh of peace. They are very helpful, as is sleeping on white sheets. You wish to be healthy as you undergo great movement and change.

Having gone through these shifts, you will present a bright and sparkling countenance to a prospective employer. Your energy will be higher, and you will be a wonderful person to add to an employer's staff. No problem exists with securing the right position, Joan; it is merely a matter of accessing it, which you will do from the depths of the spiritual "groundedness" you will feel. You will see that this is the right work over another.

Ever try your hand at painting, Joan? Now is a good time to see what happens, to see what this form of expression will let loose from your heart.

The new space is shiny and new—of that you can be sure. By shiny and new, we mean that you will feel a newness to it that is good for your life. The sun streaming in is positive, as we said to the counsellor. We think the fact that you are able to feel the new living environment and manifest just what you need and desire is a great demonstration of how far you have journeyed. Actually see the new space; foster that image in your mind, for it will help the manifestation to occur more fully.

As well, a calm, loving, peaceful relationship in your life is something that you will need to grow in your mind for it to manifest. At this time, the manifesting of a relationship is more than you can truly manage. You are busy with the closure of one living situation, Joan, so there is no space inside for the creation of the new relationship, or even a revamping of an old one. All you need to do is whatever needs to be done at this time in your life, and to keep your heart open for a loving relationship that you know is good for your soul and life forever.

Not clear? We will try again. We are saying that you are

clouded. Your vision is clouded by what is going on, a transition that has not yet concluded. We are suggesting that you focus on the transition, on the movement and change, and keep your heart open. That way, you will not be closed to whatever is possible. In the realm of ultimate possibilities, anything is possible, Joan, so keep your heart, mind, and soul open. All you need is openness, and you are able to stay open, which is a good way of being.

We hope that these few things will enable you to move forward, Joan. We hope that you will bring joy to the centre of your life again after shedding through tears the sadness you held in your heart. It's time now to move the tears and say goodbye to the sadness. However, it is a process and a journey to do so. It is not a thing that you say and then expect immediate results. We hope that this will be clear, Joan, for it is a great key to your happiness. Thank you.

Surrender Summary

When my angel said, "I am your angel, and I'm with you," a great and powerful love surrounded me. I was not alone. This was unconditional love, which for me is another word for compassion. Receiving unconditional love reinforced my understanding that when you express love, kindness, and truth, they intertwine and remain inseparable, just as time and space do. Receiving this love expanded my awareness that hurting each other, killing creatures unnecessarily, or hurting Earth's fecundity by our actions expresses fear, greed, and living life from a platform of loss. The absence of love is fear. The absence of fear is love. Living in the arms of love is exemplified in the timeless song, "What a Wonderful World," written by Bob Thiele and David Weiss, and made famous by Louis Armstrong. The lyrics compassionately state that when we say hello to each other, we are really saying, "I love you!"

After I emotionally surrendered to an unseen and unknown force by asking for help, I received help instantly. I was immediately drawn to take the perfect writing course that showed me how to make a workable plan for any writing project. I was also led to seek a counsellor, who immediately directed me to live a path of purpose. My body and mind were suffused with enough strength to withstand any negativity in my environment. My decisiveness was marvellous. If my body had allowed it, I would have written night and day. It was exhilarating to finally be free from the psychological chains that bound me to old habits.

Throughout the writing of *Spirit Love*, as I intuitively perceived ideas, my thoughts were aflame with the assurance that my words were inspired by listening to my angels and guides. As Stephen King said in his book *On Writing*, I also felt that I was taking dictation from a god or goddess energy, my angel, or my spiritual guides. During this period, I would spontaneously type the words "thank you" in response to the seamless insights I received and which flowed into a natural and meaningful order on the page. It was a transcendent experience. My creative drive, which had been dormant from lack of the right stimuli, emerged again to heal the psychic pain I felt by not following my dreams.

The love I feel and the intuitive ideas I receive from my angel and guides teach me that their help is given to me in unchangeable currency. It is constant. They led me to live a life made profound with meaning, and I experience the sublime ecstasy of living in a loving circle on Earth, connected with my angel and guides.

How Unhappy Was I?

Who, within the circle of my friends and family, noticed how unhappy I was? My husband kept saying to me that I looked so unhappy. I replied, "Yes. And you're making me unhappy! You don't support me. You never encourage me to write."

My unhappiness was a definite drain on our relationship. I wanted so desperately to blame him when I did not write each day. I kept looking outside myself to quell the unhappiness I felt inside. I knew that I needed my spirit to always remain buoyant so I would have the energy to complete my projects. I did not know how to balance my everyday activities with a writing life.

Much later, upon examining my feelings, I discovered my heart telling me that my unhappiness stemmed from not pursuing my writing dream. I needed to fulfill my passion to make a difference in the world by writing.

I examined the shadow side of my personality, which always eagerly reacted to others' wants and supported their desires before my own. This left me with little emotional and physical energy to fulfill my own needs. I uncovered my slavishness to appease and, therefore, please other people. I had no time to acknowledge and act on my dream.

Emotional Impediments

When I suddenly began to write about my adult life, I knew that writing was the occupation I was most passionate about. This ambition was too daunting for me to consider, as I was married and a mother of two young sons. I believed I could only be either a wife and mother or a writer. I could not be both. I chose to be a wife and mother, and I held myself back emotionally from writing for twenty-five years. During those years I would write only short essays and poems only when my spirit moved me to do so. When I did get the chance to write consistently after my children had grown, I discovered my commitment to start writing again was weak, and I had developed a fear of writing. Some days I struggled to write, and other days I did not write at all. I was devastated by these realizations.

Do What I Say I Want to Do

My family wanted me to do what I said I wanted to do. But acting on my desires required me to have clarity in my vision and faith in my ability. The struggle to achieve this raged within me, unknown to others. I masked my feelings with sarcastic jokes. Deep in my soul, I felt that I was a failure. My dream was too scary to contemplate. I was dreaming a big dream. What if I could not deliver?

My reactions became inappropriate. I wrongly interpreted suggestions about my writing from my loved ones as criticism. I felt no lasting joy in my life. I was letting myself down by approaching writing from the sidelines, making forays into writing that led nowhere. I needed to take a leap of faith and work on a specific project. I had to embrace the belief that following my dream was the purpose of my life. No other interest has enthralled me as much as writing. It is like the electric passion of first love.

My life and my dream are one. I am continuously in the flow of my life as I follow my dream. My happiness is grounded in the complete faith that what I am doing is helpful to others who are searching to ground their dream in reality, lifting them to the great heights of their vision.

Taking Down the Barricades

A major barrier to fulfilling my dream of writing was a lack of belief in myself—a belief that I could get up every morning and write.

I blamed a lot my unhappiness over not pursuing my dream on my lack of critical thinking. Life was an either-or proposition for me. When personal problems delayed the completion of *Spirit Love*, I could not imagine finding a solution or compromise. I could have chosen to step over or go around each obstacle. If writing steadily every day were my goal, I would have found solutions to any delays that interrupted my work.

One of the tenets I hold is respecting other people's viewpoints and allowing them the freedom to be who they are. In the midst of applying these fine principles to others, I forgot to apply them to myself first. This realization comforted me and gave me the impetus to restart my writing project.

Another reason for avoiding writing was that I hadn't answered some subliminal yet powerful questions lurking in my head. They became clear one day:

- Why am I writing?

- For whom am I writing?

- What would I be writing about?

All these questions gave me the same clear answers: *everything we do is about giving and receiving love.*

The answers immediately gave me the impetus to claim a space of my own in my home. This was a declaration of writing!

With reverence I placed all the writing tools I needed in that area. On my desk I placed a reading lamp, a computer, notepads, and pens. I added items to contemplate from nature, such as small rocks collected from Caribbean and Scottish beaches and a quiet water fountain. In the vase on my desk, I placed a bunch of lightly scented, deep yellow daisies that reminded me of the sun. I taped inspirational quotes from my angel cards and excerpts taken from sessions with my spiritual guides to the sides of my computer. In this place I prayed before I wrote and gave thanks for the inspiration I was receiving each day. I was having a daily spiritual experience with my angel and spiritual guides. This area became my altar to creativity, where my stilled mind and clear intentions could unfold into reality.

I became alert to the constant stream of intuitive ideas I was receiving from my guides and angel. I turned these meditative musings into the content of *Spirit Love*. Doing this caused my self-centred, egotistical, and overly emotional behaviours to regress, and my thoughts alighted on more appropriate ideas. My desires became clearer to me. I was transcending everyday life.

The Desire to Achieve My Dream Is Always Present

If my mind and body would permit it, I would write night and day. Each day, I keep my mind focused on completing *Spirit Love* by repeating these daily activities:

- In a special book I note ideas and inspirations I receive throughout the day.

- I keep my relationships strong and my mind calm with loving thoughts.

- I exercise my body and become fit by walking, playing tennis, or swimming.

- I eat organic, unprocessed food and drink filtered water.

- I arrange my surroundings harmoniously.

- By taking all these actions, I am putting my thoughts in order and keeping my body healthy so that my mental and physical energy remain high.

Here is a suggestion for the reader:

Pay attention to the intuitive ideas you receive. Note what actions you took that tell your spiritual guides and angel that you are paying attention by following their suggestions.

Once you become skilled at listening to and acting on your intuitive ideas, your dreams will begin to show glimmers of reality. You will have no more questions about their priority in your life. A bubble of joy and enlightenment will live inside you that can lift you off the ground to keep you soulfully happy. Remember that you are not alone. Thank your angel and spiritual guides, who are with you at all times.

The gospel of St. Matthew said that all you have to do is have faith the size of a tiny mustard seed. The ceaseless energy of your desires, combined with consistent actions, will develop your ideas from concept to reality.

You will be bathed in the light of positivism and possibility. You will experience a changing state of consciousness and feel compassion for yourself and all others. This is another way of saying you are in love with yourself and others. It shows the purposeful way in which you live your life.

How Does Writing Make Me Feel?

I am swimming in the flow of my deepest purpose when I am writing. Writing is my reason for being.

The simplest words can deliver an emotional impact that can clarify the intended outcome.

For example, a line of dialogue in a film about undeclared love can startle the viewer by suddenly illuminating a path to happiness for the characters. In the movie *Jerry Maguire*, the words, "Shut up; you had me at hello!" were splendidly uttered by Renée Zellweger to Tom Cruise while he was desperately trying to convey his true feelings about her with half-formed sentences.

The ability of words, written or spoken, to change outcomes by expressing difficult emotions in constructive ways opens up a magnificent possibility to change hostile attitudes between people to loving ones. This is my quest.

An Awareness of Self-Love

The basis of my hidden unhappiness was that I was not following my passion. I was unaware that loving me was an essential precondition of following my passion. Self-love was a foreign concept, as my upbringing had emphasized loving others, which was a wonderful way of interacting with family members that I naturally extended to loving others beyond the family. This habit has lasted throughout my life. But as an adult, I needed to look at my needs as a separate person. Growing up, my siblings and I heard judgmental words about our inabilities to complete some tasks. Hearing them restrained me from practising the fail-and-succeed habit necessary for developing and completing writing projects. If I had been conscious of loving myself first, writing would have been at the centre of my life. I judged myself harshly for my failure to write every day. More seriously, after a few days of not writing, I felt that I had lost the ability to do so. I finally understood that by acknowledging my strong aspects, such as having the determination to always do the right thing, and my weak aspects, such as not loving myself enough to follow my dreams, I could have the chance to know and love my whole self.

A Momentous Day

Hurrah! As I write, it has been one hundred days since I committed myself to being a writer. *Spirit Love* is the project that made itself known to me through my spiritual guides, and I have been writing over four hours each day for months now.

How has my family reacted? My husband tells everyone that I am a writer. My elder son, Graham, listens intently and encourages me. My younger son, Michael, is delighted for me and says I must be good at it, as he finds writing so hard to do. I ask him, "Who else has a clearer vision of my dream than me?" I expound on writing and say, "It is love and it is passion!" My brother Dean says that he is going to visualize me signing books at an event. We laughed together when I mentioned that I visualized the same event.

I believe in my heart and head that I am a writer. I am no longer hesitant to say what I do. *I am a writer!* The existential question I always had about my place in the world has finally been answered. Once again, I bring gratitude into my life with the words, "Thank you, my angel. Thank you, my guides."

A State of Readiness

Since receiving help from my angel and spiritual guides, a separate, newborn personality has emerged from my former ambiguous self. My angels and guides encourage me to conquer my fear of writing and to become conscious of what it means to love myself fully. I feel like an animal that has come out of its lair to sniff the air and, after doing so, decides that it is safe to step outside and show itself to the world. Also, my childhood view that disagreement with others is akin to betrayal has fallen away. I can now lovingly express my preference for making one choice over another without worrying that I'll be offending someone. I am fearless in the pursuit of my happiness, knowing that the words I write could set others free to be themselves.

Now, when I experience doubt, fear, anger, or sadness about writing or a relationship, I move quickly to replace those feelings or images with a vision of me dancing into the waves of my favourite beach. This is the way I expel negative thoughts and return to a loving perspective with renewed confidence. Each time I dispel these thoughts, I return to a place of certainty to carry out my destiny: to help take the world to a place of happiness and peace through my behaviour and my writing.

Three Dreams

I began to dream a lot during my transition to a new life. Here are some of the dreams I had and how I interpreted them.

First Dream

The first inspiring dream I had was of my mother, who I'd never dreamed of before. She took my hand and led me to the edge of a cliff and said, "Jump!" She was going to jump with me! This dream came at a time when my marriage of twenty-eight years seemed to be over and we needed to separate. My mother was telling me to leap into other possibilities and to not be afraid, as she was there to help me. I was comforted that she was guiding me. This gave me the resolve to work on *Spirit Love* each day. I attended computer classes and upgraded my skills to prepare myself for finding a suitable job that paid me well enough to live on my own. By then, my faith in also receiving spiritual help was unshaken and led me to take more chances. It also gave me courage to leave Toronto and live alone for four months near a beach on the island of Tobago. I wrote each day in the quiet repose of my apartment by the sea.

Second Dream

In this dream, I observed myself giving an erudite, vibrant speech. I was aware that I was portraying myself as a confident and motivating orator. I was mimicking the desires I had in the real world. I could not discern the content of the speech, but it filled me with belief in myself.

Third Dream

In the last of these powerful dreams, a fat, translucent snake was making its way, via the staircase, up to the third floor of our home. The body of the snake was beautiful and did not strike any fear into me. It filled the entire staircase, from the first to the third floor. The imposing image of the snake rising slowly to the top left me with the impression that I would keep moving ahead with my desires and reach my goals.

At the time of these dreams, we had already sold our home and, while we each looked for a new living space, kind and loving friends offered rooms in their homes and sustained us until we found our separate accommodations. These vividly symbolic dreams gave me tremendous optimism to continue making changes in my life.

Defining Moments

The first of many defining moments came when I answered these questions posed by my spiritual guides and me:

- Is my unfulfilled dream destroying my relationships and self-esteem?

- Is fear of failing holding me back?

- Am I terrified of not meeting my goals?

The answers were, of course, "Yes," "Yes," and "Yes." My guides cleared the way for me to see a new reality when I acknowledged my fears.

I acted on every idea and instinctive feeling I received. I could access this wisdom whenever I asked for direction in my writing or my life. The wisdom I received instilled in me a deep love for myself. I could no longer restrain myself from following my dream. A peaceful and confident new me emerged.

When I acknowledge my angel's and spiritual guides' help and thank them, I feel a shiver of delight that tingles about my shoulders and head. My belief in the purposefulness of life is potent. I also feel I am a powerful person because my awareness of who I am and my connectedness with all living beings is ever-present. I am humbled by this knowledge. I no longer question if I am a writer. My soul and spirit are bubbly and happy, although I know that there are life changes ahead.

These changes call upon me to examine my life and to explore the answers to these questions:

- What have I done so far in my life?

- What do I intend my future to be?

I know that I must consider how my decisions would affect others in my family. To help me decide what I should do, I ask myself this question: What would love do? And then I act with loving intent. This is not hard to do, as I surrender to love for my own good and the good of others. I infuse all possible solutions with love.

A miraculous feeling of happiness and compassion comes over me, and an untenable situation is healed. The private act of changing my attitude from anger to love reveals a peaceful solution.

My career as a homemaker ended when my sons came of age. The question I posed to myself then about my new life's purpose hung like a ghost around me, waiting to be answered. I still had not imagined life as a writer.

As the years progressed and my expectations of having a different kind of marriage did not unfold, I realized I needed help to ease my unhappiness. One evening, just before falling asleep, I implored someone for help. I mentally said, "I need help; please help me." A sudden calm ensued and, in my mind, I heard a voice say, "I am your angel, and I'm with you."

Before awakening to the unseen world of spirituality, I did not understand the need to pray for something. I believed whatever I needed to live well would be supplied by my own efforts. Although I had experienced good results from a well-developed habit of following my instincts, I did not live a spiritual life.

When I received that voiceless and comforting reply, my nascent belief that something "out there" was waiting to be known awakened me from a deep sleep. I was eager to learn more about the unknown world.

Whether we are in crisis or not, if we open ourselves to the unknown help that exists for us all, we can receive the abundant care and love available from our angel or spiritual guides.

We must ask for the help we need. Our minds will be illuminated with the understanding that to be fully human means much more than having a family, shelter, warmth, and food. It also means pursuing and achieving a joyful life that is filled with spirit.

There is nothing that we cannot do successfully when we imbue it with spirit's help. When I cultivate a peaceful green space and plant peonies that will soon be blooming with large, delicate, and heavenly scented flowers, I am tending to the love I have for my fellow human beings through this act of compassion.

Each time I reject and transcend an unloving thought, I feel a tingle around my shoulders and head. This is a confirmation from my angel or higher spirit that I did the right thing. From this response alone, I become more aware of spirit's continuous involvement in my life.

All my actions emanate from a foundation of love. I know that all the tiny acts of love that I take throughout the day are permeated with holiness.

Defining Moments for You

Here are some statements and questions that can also give you defining moments.

1) *This is my list of unfulfilled dreams:*

_____

_____

_____

2) *Are unfulfilled dreams affecting my relationships and self-esteem?*

_____

_____

_____

3) *Is fear of failure holding me back?*

_____

_____

_____

4) What can I do _now_ to revive those dreams?

_____

_____

_____

5) When I pursue my unfulfilled dreams, how will my future be changed?

_____

_____

_____

6) As I make the decision to revive my dreams, I ask myself, "What would love do?" to address my concerns that changes in my routine will affect my relationships. All my future actions will be based on continually asking and answering that question.

7) I have to make a decision about

_____

_____

_____

8) Love of myself and others would make me take this action to protect my relationships with family and friends:

_____

_____

_____

An Abundance of Inspiration

When I was told by my spiritual guides to just sit and begin writing, and that the project would make itself known to me, I trusted them and did exactly that. The spiritual world became real to me. The three sessions with my guides filled me with confidence about what I could undertake. Their assessment of my fears was accurate. I was now floating in the spiritual world that I'd always felt existed and receiving advice from that world. It seemed full of endless possibilities and with its own energy that inspired my writing to appear from nowhere. My spiritual muse was present.

Synchronistic events began to happen immediately. All I had to do was ask for help and be attuned to the answers when they came. The draft of *Spirit Love* was written quickly and smoothly, with no writer's block. In great leaps, *Spirit Love* moved forward as I consistently received inspiration to write words instilled with my exact intentions. As with the elegant intelligence of mysterious forces in the universe, this abundant inspiration contained precise ideas that I used. Again, I was moved to tears of gratitude throughout the writing, and I silently repeated, "Thank you" to my unseen helpers, my angel and spiritual guides.

My Built-In Radar and My Knowing

"Yes!" my spiritual guides said. "Yes!" Although the passage was rough, as I was lonely and heartbroken, I did not feel alone. I felt no panic—only calmness in my mind and body. Doors opened, and I received practical and emotional help from my family and friends. Paths were lit for me to follow my ideas. I was guided to buy the right home for myself with the split proceeds from the sale of our home. My husband lent me half of the down payment I needed to close the sale. Later, as we fell in love with each other again, it became a shared cost. We instinctively set a beautiful emotional tone between us. He comes to look after me when I am ill with the flu. We are inseparable in spirit because of our love for each other. Our hearts are still in love although we are apart and cannot foresee that our marriage will mend its tear. A friend wants me to start dating, but I do not give myself permission.

Occasionally, I become morose about a problem in my life because I have momentarily forgotten to ask for help from my angel and spiritual guides. At these times, I remember to obliterate the voice of the ego, with its negative messages, and to reaffirm that I am not alone.

I act only from what I feel in my heart as I heed the prompts of my higher spirit or higher being. We are one, and I act in unison with that knowledge. My inner core vibrates with happiness.

Since awakening to receiving loving, angelic, and spiritual help, I have increased my expressions of love and compassion to others and to everything that exists. By my words and actions, I show my heart's tenor to the world.

I am delirious with happiness because I always have intuitive help.

Thank you, my angel and my spiritual guides—the energy being of my higher self or higher spirit.

List of Synchronicities

I Seek and Find Help

I asked for help from the universe and I was introduced to my angel. I embrace the idea that I am not alone, and that I have help available to me at all times. It is an awesome and emotional experience.

I Knock and the Door Opens

Each time I simply think of something I need, either for writing or for my life, help appears in some form. I become accustomed to listening to my intuition, seizing opportunities that give me what I need. The help I receive is practical, emotional, and loving.

I am humbled by the divine help I am receiving. I am thankful to the universal energy that brings it to me.

Here is a list of pivotal help I received. The help was both professional and personal.

- I sought and found a spiritual counsellor and received, in great detail, practical ideas from my spiritual guides.
- I sought and found the perfect home situated near water and close to beautiful and peaceful surroundings.
- I received help to find the right job-retraining program and was offered a job soon after completing it.
- I sought and found the right writing association. I made many new writing friends, and I was motivated by various invited speakers at the monthly meetings to improve and complete my projects.

PART 2

Your Self-Examination

Using Your Talents

We all know where our interests or talents lie. Use these suggestions to start developing them. You can begin to live a life filled with meaning.

LIST YOUR INNATE TENDENCIES, INTERESTS, OR TALENTS.

Examples: Writing prose and/or poetry; running or doing general fitness exercises; studying history; taking care of animals; dancing; singing on stage; coaching or teaching; or studying anthropology

_____

_____

_____

COMBINE TWO OF THESE INTERESTS AND DEVELOP THEM.

Examples: studying history and anthropology; teaching others how to take care of animals

_____

_____

_____

Now identify possible careers and gain mastery of them through study and practice. Choose the combinations that will give the most meaning to your life because your intention is to do what you love.

Who Are You?

The initial responses to everything that occurred in your early life are recorded in your psyche or mind. These responses were influenced by your parents, caregivers, and societal norms. Later, your peers had qualities that you emulated, and you were shaped by both what you learned and the reactions of others. Some influences provided great examples of how to live. As you became older and your knowledge of your identity solidified, you questioned the opinions others had of who you were.

Remember how thrilled and excited you were when you glimpsed reminders of your authentic self. Return to these memories and imagine a new future for yourself.

Welcome and embrace everything about the way you think and what you do that makes you soulfully happy. Continue this discovery of your true self until it matches what is engraved onto your soul.

As if you were an archaeologist, dig at the site of your early years and gently brush away the dust, dirt, and small stones that have stuck so long to you and hidden the essence of your beauty. When you have gathered all the broken bits of your lost dreams, fit the parts together again with love and care. See the whole of you take shape. Bring to light the beautiful and complete treasure that you were when you were first made. And feel yourself healed by this love of yourself and, also, by the love from the unknown and unseen force that has ignited your life.

Maintain a true confidence in yourself after regaining your identity. This is fundamental for quarrying the right materials to build your dream.

The strength you need to open the door to your dreams is derived from connecting to your higher spirit. We all hear that small voice that compels us, mostly in times of crisis, to make one decision instead of another. This is the pillar you can lean on to help you make the right decision.

Have patience with yourself as you struggle on this journey of self-discovery. Perseverance will lead you to answer deeper questions about your purpose in life.

You will have a growing awareness that everyone is connected to everyone else because we all have the same desires and impetus for seeking self-fulfillment as you do.

When you decide that fulfilling your dream is the main purpose in your life by saying, "This is my dream," a creative force will begin to stir from its slumber.

After you discover and reclaim your real self, your intuition will grow stronger and you will have access to continuous information relating to your dream. Your intuition will propel you to act. You may be led to a particular course of study or action, or to a person who will help you open the door to your dream. It can be as simple as being taught how to organize your work. Once you see the road ahead clearly, be prepared for the roller coaster ride of your life.

After you study the gurus in your field, gain mastery of your particular passion, and do the substantial, patient work needed to seek out your authentic self, magic and spirit will enter your life. The magic of synchronicity will be noticeable, and the spirit of your work will make itself known to you, as it did to me. Your angel and spiritual guides are always present. Acknowledge their help with words of gratitude. They will acknowledge your awareness of them, as they do with me.

Avoiding the Void

Practical Steps

Examine how you are currently living your life. Are you living a life that is a copy of someone else's? Does your life consist of continuous reactions that keep you in a stagnant place? Or are your decisions made by a free will after considering the results of choices you make? Sometimes our first answers are not accurate. If you feel that there is a void in your life, begin to explore the reasons for that void. Here are some actions I took that helped me move forward with my quest:

- I attended brief therapeutic sessions where I answered incisive questions and acted upon the answers.
- I asked for help from an unknown source, and my angel answered.
- I sought a spiritual counsellor and was introduced to someone whose gift connected me with my spiritual guides—the energy of my higher spirit. I acted on the precise suggestions they gave me, which changed my writing habits.
- I read inspiring books that increased my knowledge of the world and instructional books on writing. I listened to motivational tapes that helped me retain a focus on all my writing projects.
- Finally, each day I asked questions of my angel and spiritual guides and listened for their answers through intuitive prompts. Then I acted on their suggestions. My connection with them is strengthened as I flex

my spiritual muscle daily.

Allow yourself to use the help you are receiving to slay or keep at bay the fiery dragons of your egotistical mind, which wants to keep your dreams in disarray.

A crystal-clear truth will eventually emerge to let you know about the higher purpose behind achieving your dream. It will give you an unobstructed view of the new direction you must take. It will be an unforgettable moment of conviction.

You are not alone in your angst about the meaning of your life. Come to the place in your heart where you honour yourself by honouring your unearthed dreams and aspirations. Lovingly share your creative gifts with the world. Deep soul happiness will be your constant companion and will grow from a tiny pinpoint of light to an ever-present sun.

Name Your Dream

Describe Your Goals and Steps

Name your dream by describing your goals using simple words. Keep refining the words to achieve a fixed but fluid representation of your true desires. Visualize different uses for your final product or service. For example, I have visualized *Spirit Love* as a meditative book, an audiobook, and a children's book.

Make achieving your dream the highest priority so that it is a shining beacon in your life. In order of importance, list all the steps you need to take. Each step will contain a goal in itself. You are developing the tenacity required to achieve your dreams.

Imagine accomplishing your dream by taking all these actions. Thoughts are an energy form that affects what you will accomplish. Do not be afraid of feeling emotional when you take these steps; according to Dr. Deepak Chopra, emotion is really energy in motion.

An Act of Intent

Organize Your Space

Locate a space within your home where you can begin to work on your dream. Discuss with your family or roommate your reasons for wishing to have exclusive use of this space and negotiate a mutually pleasing arrangement. This discussion will make your intentions clear.

Reserve your bedroom for sleeping and for meditating on and visualizing your ultimate desires.

Paint the space with a favourite colour and hang a painting that features colours you love. Place a beautiful vase containing even one flower on your desk. Nearby, place a beloved quotation. Add a sparkling water feature with small stones or something similar to keep you connected to nature.

Permit this new space to inspire a continuous outpouring of your creativity, where you receive inspired ideas that show you how to manifest your dreams.

Focus Your Desire and Intention

When I began writing the first draft of *Spirit Love,* I still didn't understand why I had been unable to write previously. My writing came from having a pure faith in myself to do the work, instilled in me by my spiritual guides. As I continued to write, I understood that life is given to us with magnificently pure intentions. We are supplied with a pristine slate upon which to draw our visions and project our instinctual feelings. We are urged to create a happy life for ourselves and for others.

Our upbringing teaches us that the world can be a punishing place if we do not conform to the prevailing customs and standards of behaviour; the world is a place where we can be easily taken advantage of and where we pay dearly for our transgressions. Our parents and caregivers naturally want us to survive the dangers to our continued existence that seemed to be lurking everywhere. Their cautions prevent our youthful selves from believing that our independent desires can be achieved.

Our free will to fashion our own lives is inadvertently hijacked by this training, as our brain creates its own connections, because of our actions, about what we can or cannot do. This brain programming can be changed only when we choose to uncover the truth about ourselves. We can then live our lives according to our original map, which still retains our undeclared dreams, by taking new actions. This map is the essence of who we are. It summons the flashes of inspiration required to fulfill our driving need to create a blissful life. It makes us aware that our dreams are achievable. They can be as close as a snowflake blowing in our face during a blizzard or, if we lose our focus, as distant from us as someone living on the far side of the Earth.

I intensified the focus on my dream of being a writer. My view of life expanded, and I saw others as tender, vulnerable beings who were also trying to make their dreams come true.

I refused to allow the fear of failing and my preoccupation with pleasing others to interfere with pursuing my dream. Previously, these self-defeating thoughts and acts had defined my existence and prevented me from moving forward. I no longer felt like an unwitting victim.

I combined my passion to write with my intention to do what would give me the result I wanted. I paid attention to the choices I made. I became a seeker of knowledge in my field of interest.

Your Body and Emotions in Balance

A mind that can perceive, control, and evaluate its emotions, and use them to guide its thinking and actions is an emotionally intelligent mind. An emotionally intelligent mind and a healthy body are in a symbiotic relationship with each other. The most beautiful and balanced work you produce will come from the harmony between your mind and your body. As you adjust your thinking to create this harmony, the journey you take to achieve your dreams will be joyful.

Always be aware of how your body feels, and compare it to your emotional state. Change your emotions if you need to. Delay taking an action until doing it will affect you and others in a loving way. Our body informs us of the nature of our thinking. Maintain an optimistic mind and steady physical energy. This will allow you to live a productive and ecstatic life.

If you prime your mind daily by choosing only positive thoughts that can resolve your problems, you allow your mind to receive a cascade of ideas. You may use some of these ideas to develop and manifest your inner desires. Similarly, you can prime your body daily with physical activities you love. You can produce a positive tandem between mind and body.

Balance Equals Energy

According to Dr. Deepak Chopra's book, *Boundless Energy*, our thoughts, negative or positive, stimulate a corresponding release of chemicals called neuropeptides. The type of neuropeptide released from our brains depends on whether the thought or feeling is positive or negative. If you experience anxiety caused by negative thoughts, you may crash your car; if you are in love, you may jump up and down on a couch because you are delirious with happiness and have abundant positive thoughts. The receptors for these chemicals are located in our nervous, digestive, and immune systems and our brains, hearts, lungs, and kidneys. We experience their negative or positive effects in our body, which then affect our energy level, mood, and creativity.

I preserve the tandem between my mental and physical energy by looking at everything from a loving perspective. This creates billions of positive thoughts for me. When the memory of a bad experience turns my mood into a negative one, I quickly replace that memory with one of a joyful experience, like being at the beach or dancing in my living room. The deep happiness and calmness I feel from the release of negative thoughts restores my equilibrium. My balance returns, and so does my energy.

Maintaining the Passion of Your Dream

Throughout your journey, it is vital to sustain the early passion you felt for your dream by creating a prototype of what you imagined it to be—a physical manifestation of what you conceived in your mind's eye. The prototype or model should contain minute details and features that will make it beautiful and stand out as an original creation. Allow the model to occupy a place of prominence in your work space. I constantly imagined *Spirit Love* as a book. I painted a prototype of the actual book cover complete with its working title, *Dreammaker*, prominently displayed on a yellow front cover. I hung it in my writing space. My dream of writing beautiful and impactful words was always present in my consciousness. Listen to the small voice within you for guidance and follow its clear and gentle suggestions.

> "It is not enough to take steps which may someday lead to a goal; each step must be itself a goal and a step likewise."
>
> —GOETHE (1749–1832), GERMAN POLYMATH

Do It for Yourself

Another way to describe the process I am recommending to you in *Spirit Love* is to imagine a garden you would like to enjoy—either your backyard garden, an apartment balcony garden, or a community garden. First decide what kind of garden you want. If you have decided on a flower garden, notice where the sun and shade are, and imagine how and where you would place the plants. Imagine your favourite flowering plants—lilies, cornflowers, stocks, daisies, luscious white peonies, and English lavender clustered around you, sharing their scents with you. You may even consider planting roses if, despite their fierce and prickly beauty, you anticipate enjoying their heavenly scent.

You begin to turn your garden from a dream to a reality by tilling the soil with fertilizer and peat moss. This fertile foundation is ready to grow your combination of flowering plants, bushes, or seeds.

The steps I took, based on the advice from my guides and the intuitive suggestions from my angel, were the right ones to prepare me for writing.

While paying attention to each detail of your dream and its eventual creation, remember that loving and caring for yourself is essential to your happiness. Acknowledge the help you receive from your spiritual sources by thanking them and consistently acting on their suggestions. They are an eternal source of guidance for you and want you to flourish and live a fulfilling life. *Loving yourself enough to be who you want to be and do what you want to do also plants seeds of courage in others.* Giving joy, compassion, and love to others will become a representation of who you are.

Answer this unspoken question. Bring your vague and deeply buried fears into the light of consciousness by writing them down. Seeing them out in the open will bring you to a juncture where you realize you must ask for help to dispel them. *What are the deepest fears that are preventing you from realizing your dream?*

If you ask for help from your angel and spiritual guides to face and dismiss your fears, they will guide you with synchronistic opportunities. Trust and follow any suggestions from your inner voice or intuition. Your guides await your questions and will reveal their answers. When you receive information, disguised as a hunch or a feeling, use it to carry out the suggested actions. Doing this increases both your intuitive abilities and the spiritual help available to you. Ultimately, your projects and life will move forward in positive ways. You are not alone.

Heaven on Earth

Even if we are not aware of it, our underlying motivation is to be happy and to create heaven on Earth. We attend holy places to allow ethereal music and profound words to enter our consciousness. We go there to gaze at the architecture, the icons, and the stained-glass windows. We want to be close to the spirit and serenity residing in each of them. This eternal craving to find out how to create heaven on Earth renders us humble as we keep searching for fulfillment. We desire to live a whole life by combining our physical and spiritual selves. My heaven on earth is to maintain loving relationships with my family and friends, caring for them and having experiences with them that represent those ideals. I experience my greatest joy when I feel the presence of my angel and spiritual guides around me and know that I am not alone.

Love and Happiness

An impending separation in my marriage became a turning point in my life. I was deeply and silently sad. There was no one with whom I could share the effects of this crisis on me. I lived in limbo, unable to feel the life in each day or imagine a future. My body was frozen, waiting for my next steps. When I had experienced enough inertia and introspection, I answered questions about the deeper unhappiness I had been experiencing even before this marital crisis. As I lay on the verge of sleep one night, I was prompted spontaneously to ask for help.

The response from my angel immediately turned me away from sadness to quiet elation as I realized I was not alone. My focus shifted to thinking about what would make me very happy. It was being a writer, of course! Luckily, I also accepted advice and emotional support from my family and friends as they pushed me to imagine another future— one that I could not imagine on my own. I could now see a thrilling future filled with writing and publishing my prose and poetry. It was also clear to me that my writing must be helpful to others. That ringing happiness I felt when my angel spoke to me is always with me.

My angel's confirmation that there was a spiritual world excited me enough to seek a spiritual counsellor. I hoped that I would be able to talk with this person about the spiritual realm. Incredibly, I found someone whose spiritual gift connected me to my spiritual guides. In the midst of great sadness, their most important advice to me was, "Joan, make joy; be joyful and others will be joyful, too." They advised me to speak words of love to myself, and I discovered that I also wanted to have loving thoughts and interactions with others. Miraculously, because there was much unspoken love between my husband and me, we were reconciled after a two-year separation.

It may be that you are currently in a situation that is making it impossible for you to follow your dream. You might believe that your vision of a soulfully happy life is unattainable. Nothing is impossible when your will is strengthened by self-love. Again, listen to the silent prompts of your guides and angel. Literally follow up on their suggestions. Use the wisdom that is available to you; the intelligence that surrounds us is waiting to help. *Remember to always ask for their help. You are not alone.* This is your journey toward self-realization, the full expression of who you are.

Writing *Spirit Love* began with me sitting at my desk and allowing myself to trust what my guides had said to me. They said that a writing project would make itself known to me. Whenever I wrote, the spirit of the work was always present and inspiring. Words flowed effortlessly onto the page, and I experienced no moments of writer's block.

Loving yourself creates a loving, enlightened you—one that is sensible, serene, and confident, expressing love in every interaction with others.

I became aware of my strained relations with my teenage son. To mend this, I decided to stop our daily shouting and arguing by replacing the thought, "I wonder what he's been up to now?" with "Here comes my son, whom I love!" Our relationship returned to being a calm and happy one in an instant. It has remained that way.

Here are some questions you can answer for yourself.

- What makes you the happiest?

- Are your activities value-based or ego-based?

Answer these powerful and clarifying questions. Follow up by taking the actions that will secure your happiness. Is personal happiness that easy to achieve? Yes!

PART 3
The End

My Exhilaration

I HAVE GIVEN BIRTH TO MY DREAM OF BEING A WRITER WITH THIS book, *Spirit Love*. My feelings are joyous! I freely associate pleasure with memories of hopping about on the hot sand as I made my way into the sea at Maracas Beach, and flailing about in the cool summer water of Georgian Bay. With my arms over my head, I whooped with delight to no one in particular, "I'm in the sea! I'm in the lake!" Basic and powerful feelings of belonging are evoked in me. I am joy itself!

Do whatever it takes to nurture your feelings of self-love. Surround yourself with what makes you joyful. Begin to feel the elements of a purposeful life by following your passion. Listen to the intuitive prompts and gut feelings you receive that indicate you should make one choice over another. These messages are being sent to you from your spiritual guides and your angel. Act on their suggestions. Closeness to them will develop. You will feel loved, nurtured, and fearless in your journey through life. You will never feel alone. Your soul will sing an aria of delirious, drunken happiness.

The energy behind my dream makes me alive with an alert calmness in my mind and body. I feel as if I'm floating on a cloud as I lie in my love's arms, not knowing where the arms of my love end and mine begin. I do not feel separate from the space and the air in the room. I am a part of it, and the room has no walls. My body and the environment have integrated, and there is no separation. I cannot tell where I begin or end. I experience a creative harmony with the universe known as Tao.

Tao is the relationship between us and the universe. We feel an exquisite completeness as the order and wisdom of our lives harmonizes with the energy of the universe. This energy makes and maintains everything that exists. This is the experience of exhilaration, of Tao.

What is your experience of Tao? Hiking the south rim of the Grand Canyon? Walking the pilgrim's path, El Camino de Santiago, in Spain? Baking a batch of sublimely delicious cookies? Or gazing in awe at a billion stars on a black night in Algonquin Park?

My experience of Tao has been as varied as having dinner with dear friends, where the acceptance of each other's differences is palpable; as peaceful as digging in my garden in the quiet of an afternoon; beautifying my table with cut flowers; or growing basil and cherry tomatoes and sharing the bounty with neighbours. Or it can be as simple as spending time on my own, absorbing the unseen but felt joyfulness around me. This is when I am feeling the presence of my angel and spiritual guides with me.

I act on every intuition I receive from my spiritual guides and my angel. They are a part of my consciousness now, and I consult them without being aware of it.

I also receive help in simple ways. A book I need to read falls off the shelf, or I am drawn to visit a bookstore and a particular title catches my interest. I may hear a song that contains a message in the lyrics for me. I have seamless, involuntary, and loving connections with my spiritual guides and my angel. I am never alone.

I am given all the help I need to live a soulful life. This is what I want for you. I want you to know that you are never alone. You are loved in all ways. May your heart be full of joy and your life lived thick with purpose. *Spirit Love* is my gift to you.

With love,
Joan Chisholm

Souvenirs of the Wisdom Received from My Spiritual Guides

Here are some souvenirs of the wisdom I received from my spiritual guides during the three sessions that I had with my spiritual counsellor. They are an invaluable reference for living my life to the highest potential. The information is like a mirror held up to me and helps me to make small, decisive steps to achieve all of my dreams.

May you begin to shine like the polished diamond that you are, and when you find the deeper meaning of your life, may all of your dreams come true.

Session 1

Unconscious Fears That Hinder Our Creative Actions

- A fear of being right about our work

- A fear of not being right

- A fear of our work not being noticed

- A fear of not being published

- A fear of not selling our work

- A fear of not being read

- A fear that our creative work is not enjoyed by or useful to others

Advice about Writing

- No one writes or creates everything all at the same time.

- Resuscitate all stop-and-start projects.

- There are more reasons to write or manifest our ideas than there are reasons not to.

- Work every single day on your project, even if it is to write one word or sentence. This will keep you in touch with your creative energy, and the spirit of the work will bless you daily.

- You may not always wish to work on a particular project. Don't abandon it. The spirit of the work may be in recess. Do other writing that eases your spirit, and return to the original work.

Release the Ego

- Ego concerns keep us in a place of stagnation.

- Ego thinks there is greener grass somewhere else.

- Ego wants us to believe that there is a better atmosphere for writing or creating.

- Ego stalls us from completing our projects by letting us think that if we did not have to deal with other issues, our minds would be clear to make swift progress.

Love Yourself

- Care only what spirit says to you and how you think about you. You will be happier!

- Love yourself much, much better than you have before.

- Value yourself and take pride in yourself—just for breathing.

- Appreciate how far you are from where you were.

- Give yourself accolades for every single little thing that you do, but do not bore others with the accolade giving because that would be an exercise in ego.

- Giving yourself internal messages of love that say things like, "I love and approve of you. I am here for you, in all ways." Do this every single day upon waking.

Manifest Your Ideas

- Stay true yourself and you will feel a great sense of accomplishment. Set yourself small, achievable goals to avoid disappointment. This first goal is to get prepared with tools and nothing more.

- Writing or any other passion must be between you and your God-self or Goddess-self. Start when you are ready. Stay with it until you have moved yourself into your centre. Manifest your ideas on paper and make a prototype of your dreams to reach your internal core.

Only Believe

- Release all your feelings of low self-worth and begin at the beginning.

- Regularize and ritualize to make all things possible.

- All things are possible—only believe. Accomplish your heart's desire by putting it at the centre and praying to be helped to enable it to come into being.

Work and Pray

- Every single day, work and pray—ask your spirit to guide, bless, and help you.

- Forget about whether others will find your efforts worthy. Your work is for you and no one else.

- Every single morning, pray before you speak with others.

- Every single evening, say thank you for all that has manifested itself in your work and in your life. Every single day, keep on with work that makes sense to you.

- Do not delay or annihilate your work. Find a supportive person for positive feedback. Later, find someone to critically evaluate your work.

Session 2

Neutralize Your Working Space

- Place a fountain or other soothing talisman in your space—one that is either noisy or quiet according to your taste.

- Images in the fountain or on your talisman ought to include a sense of the sacred that appeals to you.

Daily Rituals before Beginning Your Creative Work

- Clean the fountain or your talisman.

- Change the water in your vase of flowers.

- Trim and light a beeswax candle.

- When all is ready, enjoy a sense of peace and treasure the moment.

- Complete your rituals before you speak with others in the morning.

Water

- Sip water rather than drinking it in a continuous motion.

- Water clears the physical body and makes you feel more energized.

- Water raises the vibration of the sacred in the body and in your living environment.

Pray

- Daily prayers will include everything in your heart regarding life, relationships, writing, soul, spirit, joy, appreciation, and happiness.

- Create your own prayers to suit your particular state of being. Prayers must correspond to experience, so no standard prayer will do the trick.

Contemplate

- Contemplate growing flowers or ones in vases, or a similar soothing image. This will encourage reflection so you will understand a particular bump in your creative work or life.

Create in Different Locations

- Write or create your work in different environments to create a feeling of peacefulness.

Make Joy

- Make joy for you, and you will make joy for everyone.

- Make this statement daily: "I am joyful. I am, and so it is. I am joyful, and so it is."

Session 3

Visualization

- As you create in your heart and in your spirit, so you will see manifestations in the material realm.

- Visualize the surroundings, placement, structure, and colours of your home. Visualize the details of your life and watch it come into being.

- Let the universe be your canvas. Manifest onto it all that your heart desires.

Manifestations

- Manifest your visualizations by saying to yourself, "I am now ready to accept what I am visualizing." Then watch it manifest.

Faith

- If fear dares to knock at your door, say, "I am a person of faith. I release all fear."

- Redouble your faith-based thinking and see manifestation take place.

- Have faith that all your heart desires will manifest, for that is what you came here to do.

- You have the capacity to manifest home, work, and a peaceful, loving, life companion.

- These things require no great work, for life is simple and enjoyable.

Bumps in the Road of Life

- Bumps in the road are there to overcome while you continue on your life's journey.

- When they occur, ask to be blessed with their transformation into something that secures your good.

Opening Your Heart

- You can have peace, happiness, joy, and great love. Knowing this opens the heart. This is not to be denied to you or anyone else on Earth.

Be in Love with Yourself Completely

- Love yourself in a much more close and fulfilling way than you have done before.

- Loving yourself is not a simplistic thing; nor is it complex.

Colours

- Pay attention to the different colours and their shades that you love, and wear them or have them in your surroundings.

- Visualize bringing a favourite colour into your body for five minutes to an hour. Your body will feel wonderful.

- Gaze at the yellow flame of a beeswax candles. This will clear the emotional and energy bodies.

Inner Vision

- When you discern all that is taking place in your life, the movement and change you make will enhance your inner vision.

- Your spiritual guides welcome your enhanced vision of yourself and the clearer communication between you and them that will result.

Source of Your Power

- Diligent reaching to make changes connects you with the source of your power.

- In a life-changing transition, keep your heart, mind, and soul open.

- Focus on the movement and change of the transition,

and stay open so you will not be closed to whatever is possible. Anything is possible.

Thank you, my angel, my spiritual guides—the energy being of my higher spirit.

CREATION

My soul hums a hymn,

To celebrate my creation.

My cells,

Come alive.

The intelligence in my cells comes to full alertness,

They vibrate with ecstasy.

I know,

Then,

The reason

I am Being.

—JOAN CHISHOLM

About the Author

As the middle child of a large household of eleven kids, Joan had numerous chances to practice her natural inclination to be a peacemaker.

She could easily understand both sides of an argument and was able to offer sympathetic solutions to combatants with different interests.

Her brothers and sisters remind her that when they were very young she took them to open bank accounts in their own names and bought them watches and other items to organize their lives.

It is no wonder that *Spirit Love*, written over forty years later, continues her deep caring and love of helping others. She is still giving her best efforts to others to succeed in their lives by inspiring them to follow their dreams and live ecstatic lives.

Joan lives in Toronto with her husband, two sons, and two grandchildren.

www.ingramcontent.com/pod-product-compliance
Lightning Source LLC
Chambersburg PA
CBHW032055150426
43194CB00006B/529